GW00775883

JOE SATRIANI
The Extremist

Management: Bill Graham Management
Transcribed by Paul Pappas
("Summer Song" transcribed by Andy Aledort)
Music Engraving by W.R. Music
Production Manager: Daniel Rosenbaum
Art Direction: Rosemary Cappa
Director Of Music: Mark Phillips

ISBN: 0-89524-772-0

CONTENTS

Friends

Music by Joe Satriani
and Andy Johns

4

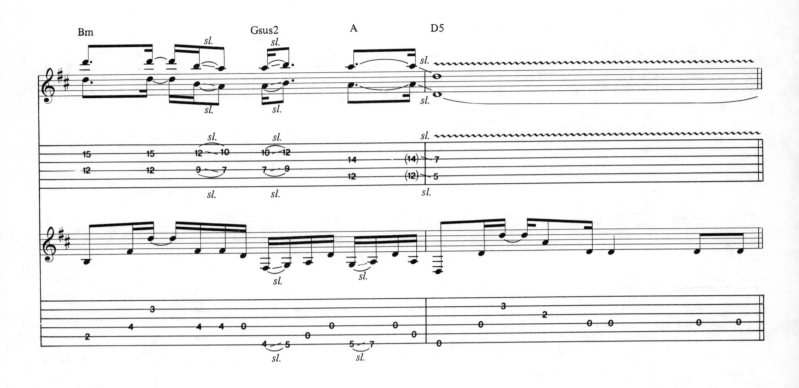

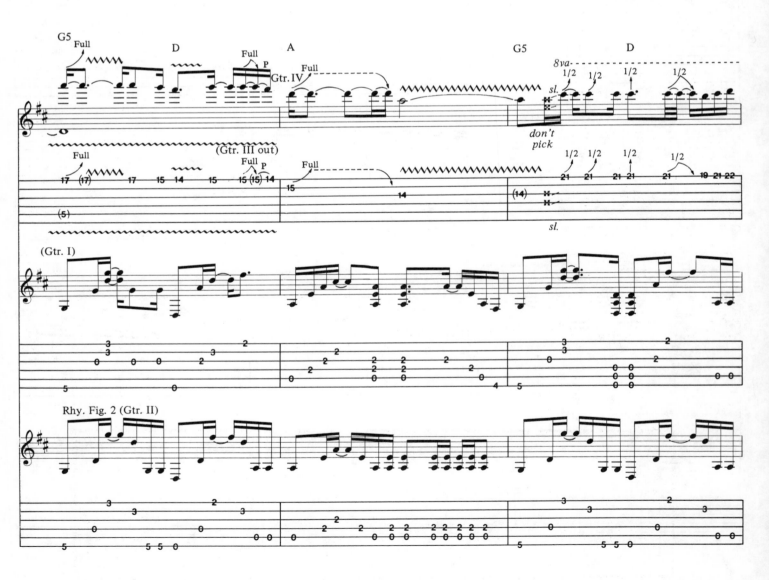

The Extremist
(Living On The Edge)

Music by Joe Satriani

Tune down 1/2 step:
⑥ = E♭ ③ = G♭
⑤ = A♭ ② = B♭
④ = D♭ ① = E♭

Moderate Rock ♩ = 94

*Gtr. I is "Nashville tuned" dobro arr. for gtr. "Nashville tuning"
is same as standard tuning except ⑥ - ③ stgs. are tuned an octave
higher than normal. Transcription written as if gtr. were tuned
normally (down 1/2 step).

*Gtr. II is 2 gtrs. & 2 "Nashville tuned"
dobros arr. for one gtr.

*On D.S., 1st chord is struck, not tied (this bar only).

*Depress bar before striking note.

17

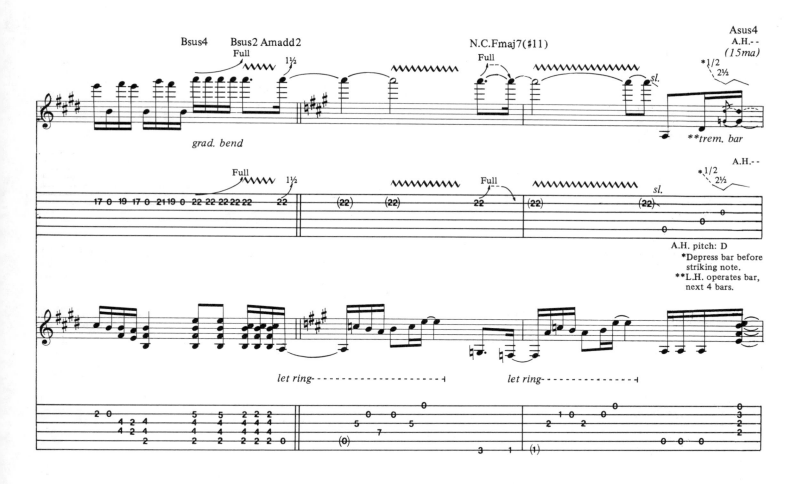

A.H. pitch: D
*Depress bar before
striking note.
**L.H. operates bar,
next 4 bars.

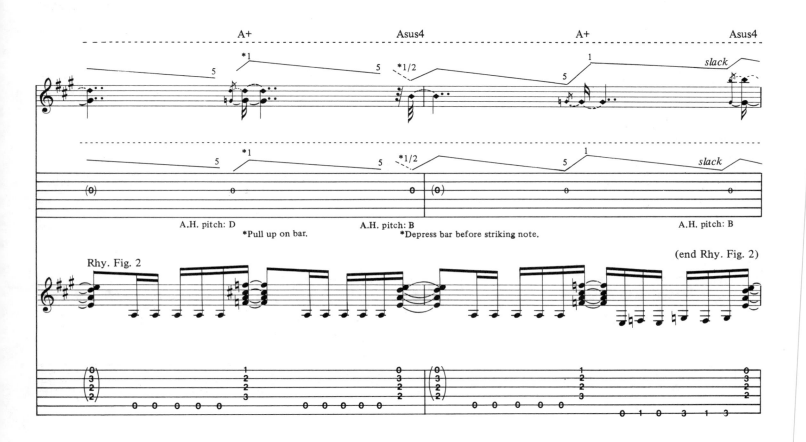

A.H. pitch: D
*Pull up on bar.

A.H. pitch: B
*Depress bar before striking note.

A.H. pitch: B

(end Rhy. Fig. 2)

War

Music by Joe Satriani

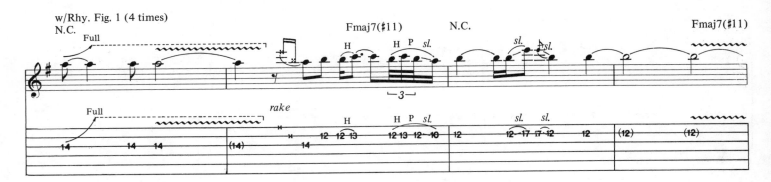

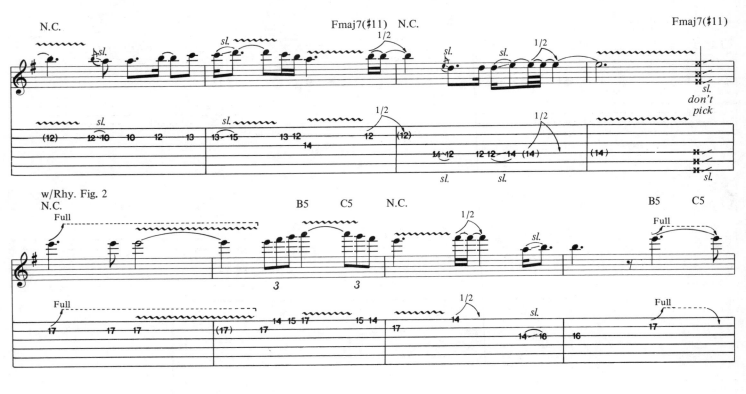

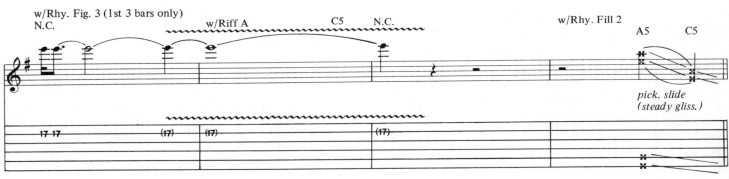

Rhy. Fill 2 (Gtrs. I & II)

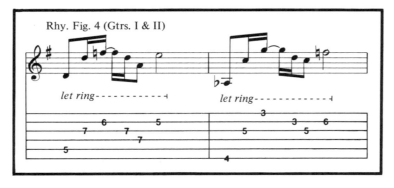

Rhy. Fig. 4 (Gtrs. I & II)

26

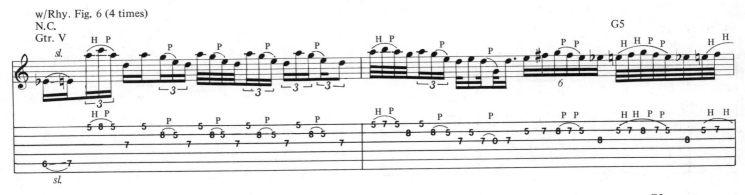

*T
*Tap w/edge of pick next 2 bars.

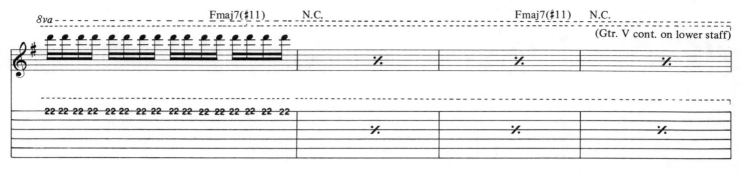

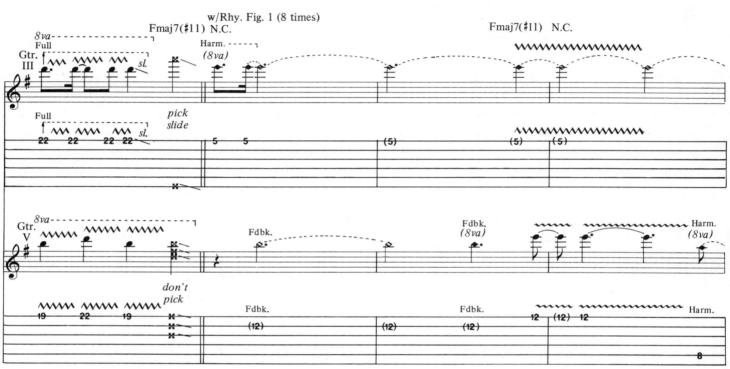

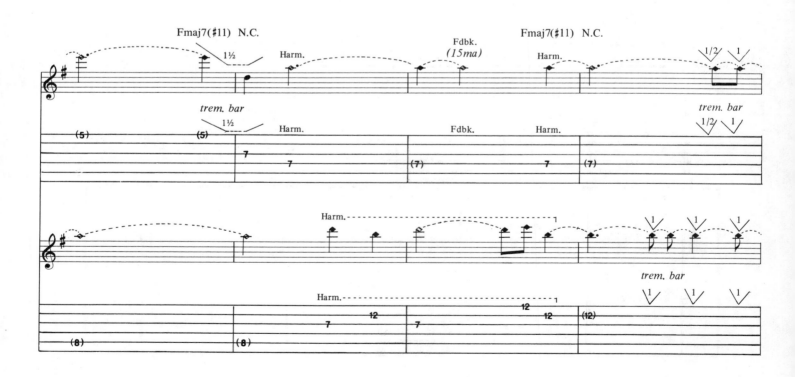

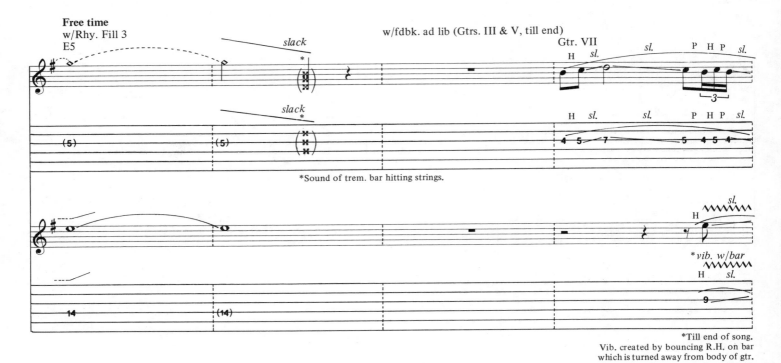

*Sound of trem. bar hitting strings.

*Till end of song.
Vib. created by bouncing R.H. on bar
which is turned away from body of gtr.

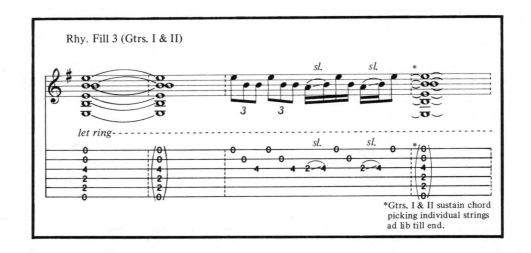

Cryin'

Music by Joe Satriani

*L.H. movement
causes open
strings to sound.

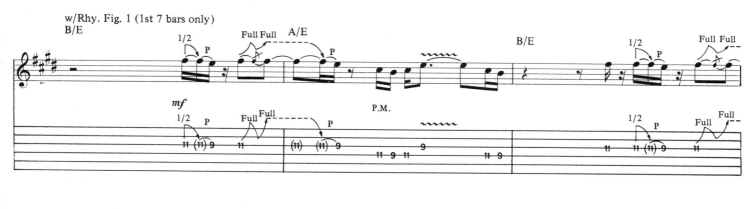

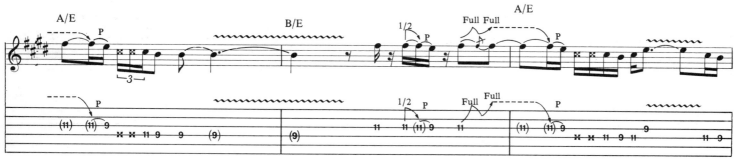

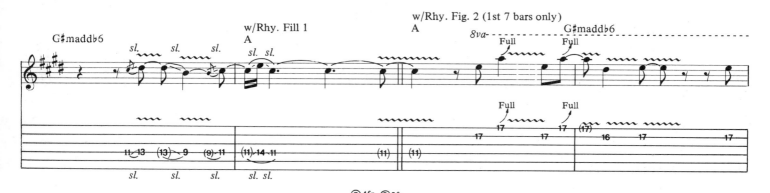

41

Rubina's Blue Sky Happiness

Music by Joe Satriani

44

50

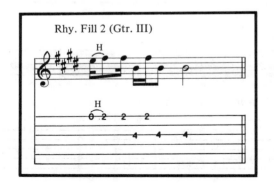

*Gtr. I notated to left of slash.

Fill 2 (Gtr. IV)

Summer Song

Music by Joe Satriani

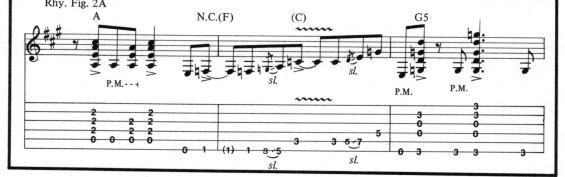

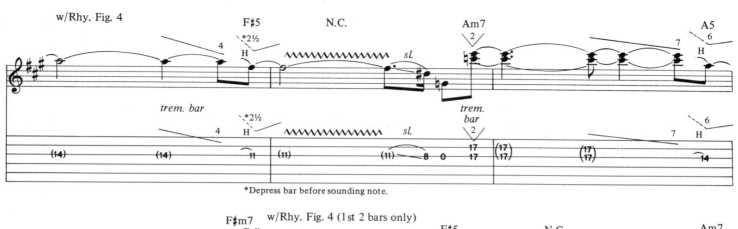

*Depress bar before sounding note.

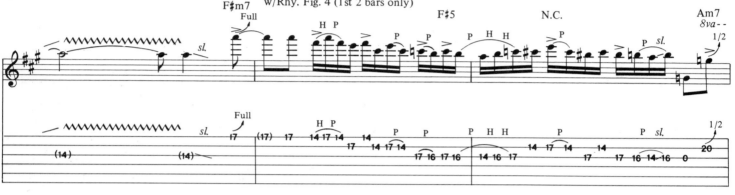

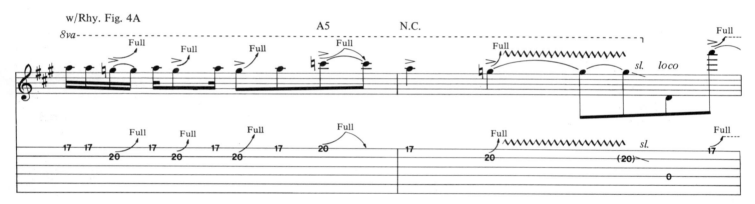

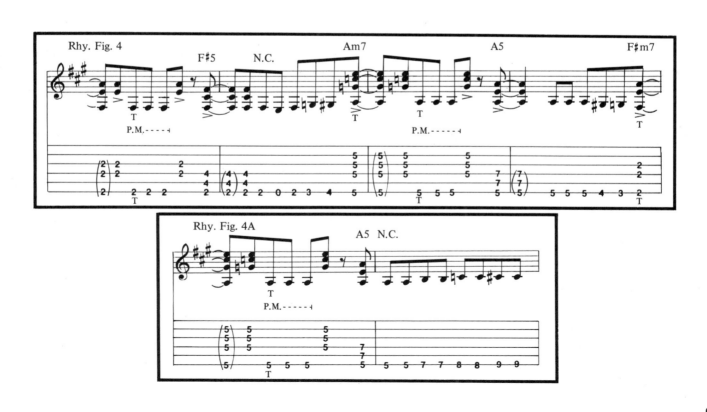

Tears In The Rain

Music by Joe Satriani

Why

Music by Joe Satriani

*Gtr. IV uses Digitech Harmony Machine. "E minor chord" preset.
Gtrs. V & VI are notes produced by harmonizer arr. for 2 gtrs.

*"Nashville tuned".

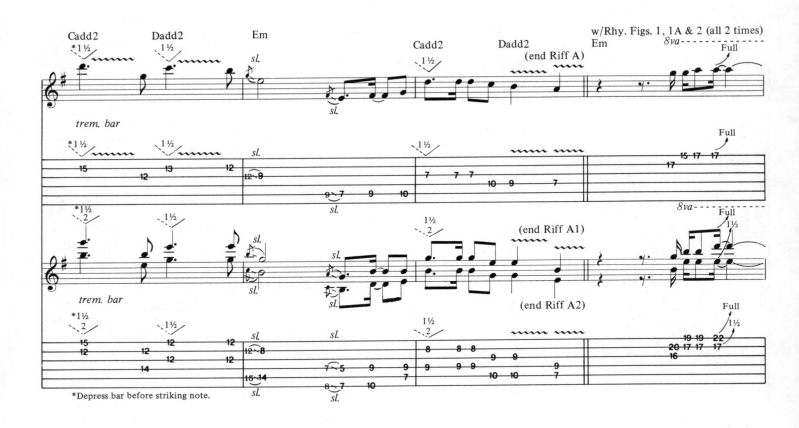

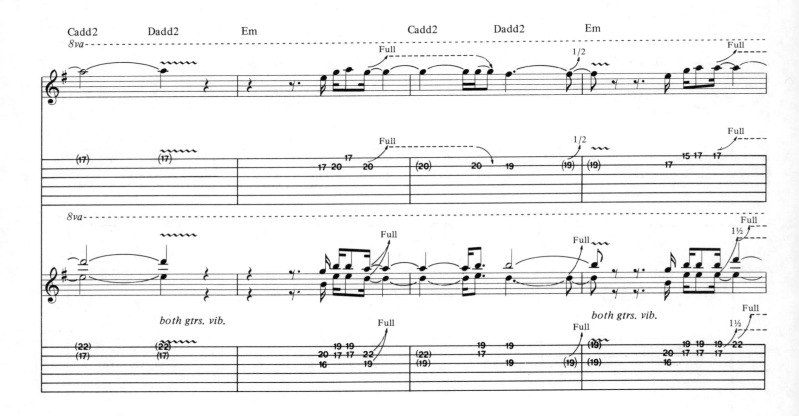

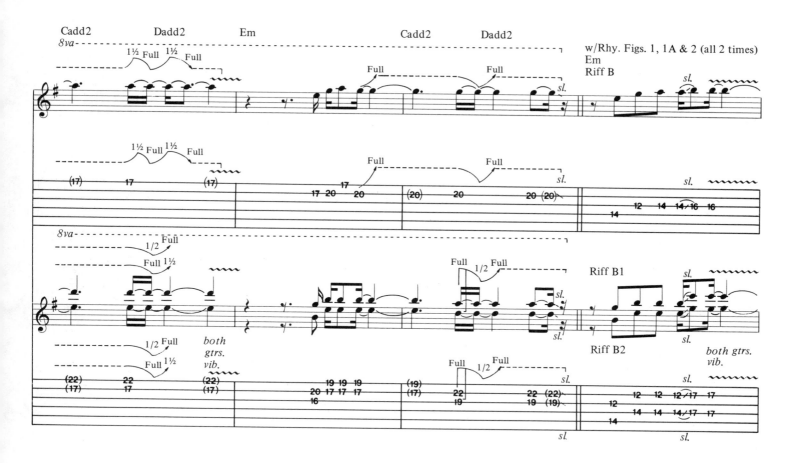

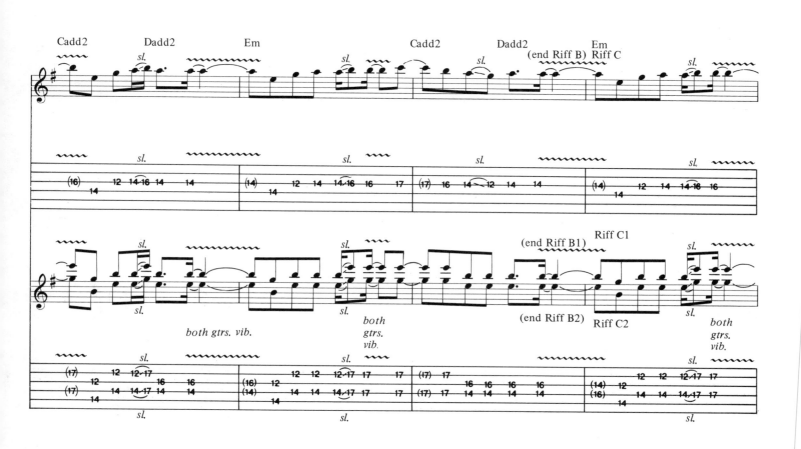

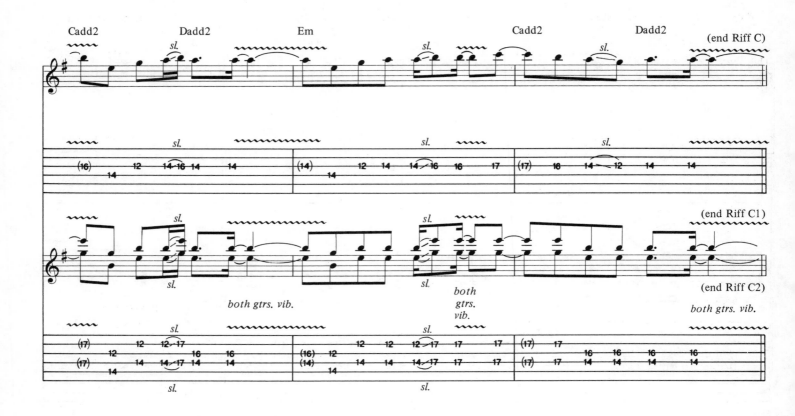

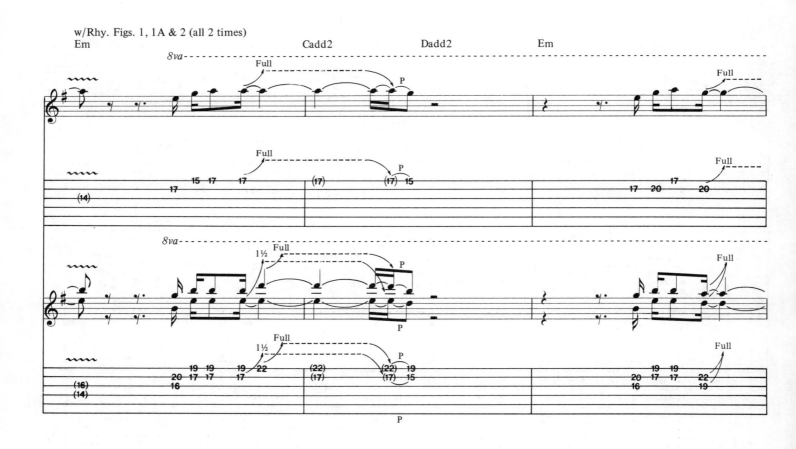

*Depress bar before striking note.

*Pull bar up & release abruptly, creating exaggerated vibrato.

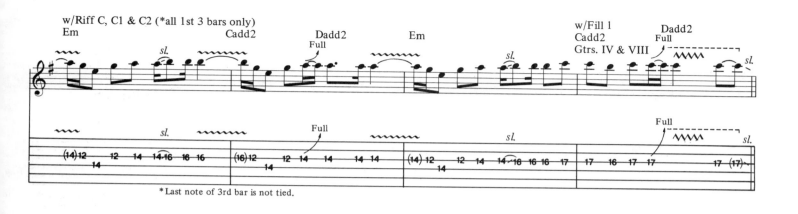

w/Riff C, C1 & C2 (*all 1st 3 bars only)

*Last note of 3rd bar is not tied.

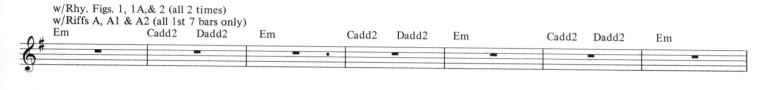

w/Rhy. Figs. 1, 1A,& 2 (all 2 times)
w/Riffs A, A1 & A2 (all 1st 7 bars only)

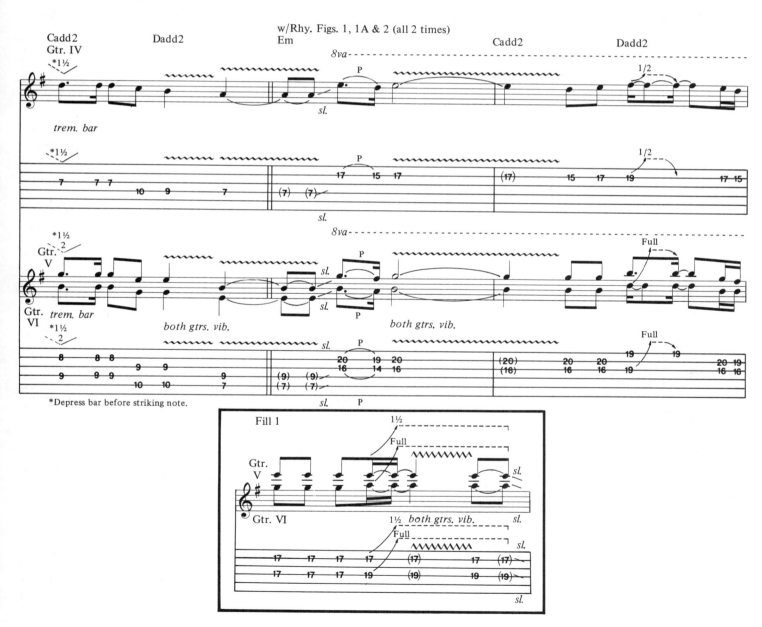

*Depress bar before striking note.

Motorcycle Driver

Music by Joe Satriani

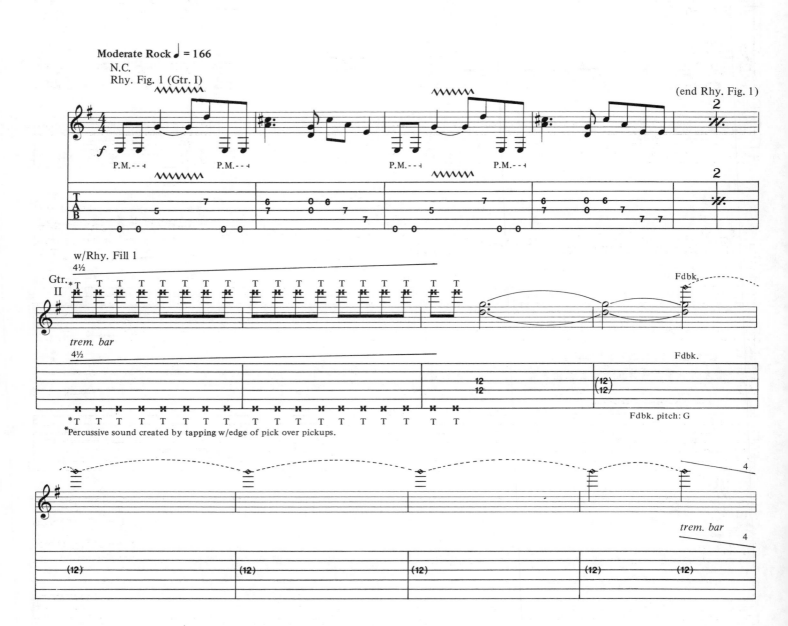

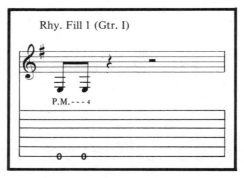

Rhy. Fill 1 (Gtr. I)

1st time Gtr. II substitute Rhy. Fill 2

*Play 1st time only.

Rhy. Fill 2 (Gtr. II)

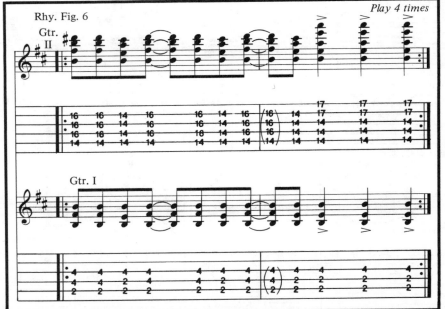

New Blues

Music by Joe Satriani

*Depress bar before striking note.

*Depress bar before striking note.

(end half-time feel)

(end Rhy. Fig. 2)

Tapping pattern continues for next 3 bars.

*Depress bar before striking note.

(end half time feel)

(end Rhy. Fig. 4)

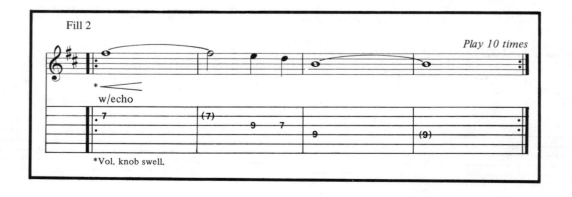

TABLATURE EXPLANATION

TABLATURE: A six-line staff that graphically represents the guitar fingerboard, with the top line indicating the highest sounding string (high E). By placing a number on the appropriate line, the string and fret of any note can be indicated. The number 0 represents an open string.

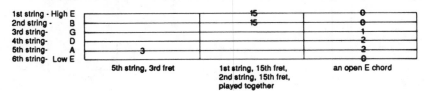

1st string - High E
2nd string - B
3rd string - G
4th string - D
5th string - A
6th string - Low E

5th string, 3rd fret   1st string, 15th fret, 2nd string, 15th fret, played together   an open E chord

Definitions for Special Guitar Notation

BEND: Strike the note and bend up ½ step (one fret).

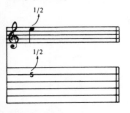

BEND: Strike the note and bend up a whole step (two frets).

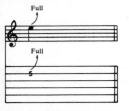

BEND AND RELEASE: Strike the note and bend up ½ (or whole) step, then release the bend back to the original note. All three notes are tied, only the first note is struck.

PRE-BEND: Bend the note up ½ (or whole) step, then strike it.

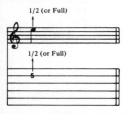

PRE-BEND AND RELEASE: Bend the note up ½ (or whole) step. Strike it and release the bend back to the original note.

UNISON BEND: Strike the two notes simultaneously and bend the lower note up to the pitch of the higher.

VIBRATO: The string is vibrated by rapidly bending and releasing the note with the left hand or tremolo bar.

WIDE OR EXAGGERATED VIBRATO: The pitch is varied to a greater degree by vibrating with the left hand or tremolo bar.

SLIDE: Strike the first note and then slide the same left-hand finger up or down to the second note. The second note is not struck.

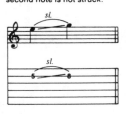

SLIDE: Same as above, except the second note is struck.

HAMMER-ON: Strike the first (lower) note, then sound the higher note with another finger by fretting it without picking.

PULL-OFF: Place both fingers on the notes to be sounded. Strike the first note and without picking, pull the finger off to sound the second (lower) note.

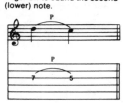

TRILL: Very rapidly alternate between the note indicated and the small note shown in parentheses by hammering on and pulling off.

TAPPING: Hammer ("tap") the fret indicated with the right-hand index or middle finger and pull off to the note fretted by the left hand.

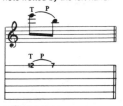

PICK SLIDE: The edge of the pick is rubbed down the length of the string producing a scratchy sound.

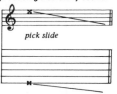

TREMOLO PICKING: The note is picked as rapidly and continuously as possible.

NATURAL HARMONIC: Strike the note while the left hand lightly touches the string over the fret indicated.

ARTIFICIAL HARMONIC: The note is fretted normally and a harmonic is produced by adding the edge of the thumb or the tip of the index finger of the right hand to the normal pick attack. High volume or distortion will allow for a greater variety of harmonics.

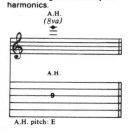

TREMOLO BAR: The pitch of the note or chord is dropped a specified number of steps then returned to the original pitch.

PALM MUTING: The note is partially muted by the right hand lightly touching the string(s) just before the bridge.

MUFFLED STRINGS: A percussive sound is produced by laying the left hand across the strings without depressing them and striking them with the right hand.

RHYTHM SLASHES: Strum chords in rhythm indicated. Use chord voicings found in the fingering diagrams at the top of the first page of the transcription.

RHYTHM SLASHES (SINGLE NOTES): Single notes can be indicated in rhythm slashes. The circled number above the note name indicates which string to play. When successive notes are played on the same string, only the fret numbers are given.